FINAL PATH

poems by

Ron Lands

Finishing Line Press
Georgetown, Kentucky

FINAL PATH

Copyright © 2020 by Ron Lands
ISBN 978-1-64662-189-7 First Edition
All rights reserved under International and Pan-American Copyright Conventions. No part of this book may be reproduced in any manner whatsoever without written permission from the publisher, except in the case of brief quotations embodied in critical articles and reviews.

ACKNOWLEDGMENTS

I thank each of these journals who first published these individual poems, some in a slightly different version.

Intima: a Journal of Narrative Medicine: "The Appointment," "Listen to the Ocean," and "Decision"
Annals of Internal Medicine: "Don't Tell Me What My Daddy Wants," and "The Language of Grief"
Journal of Palliative Medicine: "Natural Death," and "It's not the Dying"
Pulse: "Breathing the Same Air"
Chest: Journal of the American College of Chest Physicians: "Receiving Friends"
Appalachian Heritage: "Family Plot"

Publisher: Leah Maines
Editor: Christen Kincaid
Cover Art: Ron Lands
Author Photo: Kandi Hodges
Cover Design: Elizabeth Maines McCleavy

Printed in the USA on acid-free paper.
Order online: www.finishinglinepress.com
    also available on amazon.com

Author inquiries and mail orders:
Finishing Line Press
P. O. Box 1626
Georgetown, Kentucky 40324
U. S. A.

Table of Contents

The Journey 1

Stealing Home 2

Shiloh 3

Now and Then 4

The Conversation 5

Luna: Moon Goddess 6

Baby Steps 7

Decision 8

The Appointment 9

Listen to the Ocean 10

Don't Tell Me What My Daddy Wants 11

Natural Death 12

It's not the Dying 13

Last Act 15

Letting Go 16

A Promise of Rest 17

The Language of Grief 18

Receiving Friends 19

Breathing the Same Air 20

Family Plot 21

Thanks 22

FOREWARD

As a ten-year-old, I developed appendicitis. Our small-town general practitioner, a high school classmate of my dad's, took me to surgery without a specialist's consultation, an abdominal CT scan or anything else that would be considered standard in today's world. I recuperated in the hospital for a week. A nurse's aide recorded my vital signs every 8 hours on a flowsheet attached to a clipboard that dangled on a string from the foot of my bed. Every day, the nurse ripped the adhesive bandage off my surgical site and changed the gauze dressings. Before she dressed it again, she would clean my fingertips with alcohol and let me touch the thick silk sutures.

I was enchanted with the rules, the rituals, the smells, the old nurses with swollen ankles and white stockings and the seam that meandered up the back of their leg. I was awe-struck by the doctor who made rounds at random times with a pack of unfiltered Lucky Strikes in his short-sleeved clinic coat pocket and the aroma of stale tobacco smoke that heralded his entrance into my room. I felt like a member of an exclusive club when the hospital operator announced over the PA system at 9 PM that visiting hours were over and everyone had to leave the building, except us, the unhealthy and the healers.

Twenty-five years later, I came home to practice near the community where I grew up. I was privileged to treat strangers, lifelong friends and a few relatives. The blend of my vocation and avocation provided a unique lens through which I saw my patients; rich and poor, educated and illiterate, evangelical and uncertain, struggle with issues of life and death. Some of these experiences have resulted in short stories, poems and essays being published in literary and medical journals.

Almost 5 decades later, my dad, who'd had slowly progressive respiratory failure from occupational exposure and smoking that he'd stopped 40 years earlier, spent the last 4 months of his life in hospice care. Wonderful people, old friends and relatives, tried to comfort me with kind words, lines and phrases that I'd mindlessly repeated to the families of my dying patients for years. When people told me, "he's not suffering," or "He's in a better place," I bit my tongue. When I overheard the hospice staff talking to him like he was a toddler, I reminded them that he'd survived two wars and deserved to be addressed as an adult. All the while, I felt like a hypocrite.

Final Path is collection of poems, all of them personal, some of them written in response to emotions and behaviors I recognized in myself as those I'd seen in patients and their families, people I thought I'd helped in their passage along their parent's final path. It was, and still is, a journey. William Faulkner said that our past shapes our future and the present is interpreted by our memories. The doctor I wanted to be was shaped by what I learned from my experiences, my mentors in medicine and many memorable patients. The person I am now is still being shaped by the memory of my journey with my dad on his final path.

THE JOURNEY

Through the fog of war
he heard his father's call,
tracked its echo from his bunk
to the barracks steps and looked
homeward, left the California coast
in the wake of cars that passed him
standing on the highway's cold shoulder.
Starving, snowbound and absent
without leave for the 8th day,
he struggled to hear the distant drum
of a heartbeat fading into the place
where, when you go there,
angels won't bring you back.

STEALING HOME

You can see him on the front page
of the Times, August 9, 1948,
headlined "Tennessee State Champs,"
a memory in black and white
holding hostage a team of unlikely winners;
a teacher who left one arm in Germany,
banker with a blinded eye, a farmer,
fireman, and preacher who'd each lost
a step at Leyte, a carpenter, grocer and mailman,
still trapped in whiskey-soaked dreams
of German prisons. He stands in the second row,
still skinny from the war, cap off center,
cigarette dangling from a firing squad smile,
one of a team of reluctant warriors, happy
to be alive. Old men still remember
how he could drop a bunt on the baseline,
beat the throw to first, take second by surprise,
bring the crowd roaring to their feet as he rounded
third and turned toward home,
where the wind dances with the trees
and night birds fly figure eights in the streetlight.

SHILOH

We chased the Confederate Army
in a Chevrolet station wagon,
his left arm sunburned from wrist
to shoulder where he rested it
in the open window while he drove
one handed to engage the enemy
in a random battle from a war fought
a century past. We traveled down
the Sunken Road, through the Hornet's
Nest, parked by the placard next
to Bloody Pond where he lectured
without notes to disinterested sons
about hallowed ground, greater good,
freedom, the pursuit (not the promise)
of happiness. Other battles followed him
to that place where soldiers go to rest.

NOW AND THEN

What I remember now is how he tangled
his feet in the oxygen tube and tottered
backward toward the stairs, how I grabbed
and caught him by the sleeve. I remembered
then a story told in whispers, of a cool fall
evening, neighbors gathered to watch
the man he'd hired cut away the oak tree
from where it tilted over the corner
of our house, the howl of chain saws
revving into a high whine, that special blend
of sawdust, gas and oil. In the retelling,
they say the tree teetered one way and then
the other, indecisive, not yet committed
to its path, that when it fell, the world went
silent, as if God had hit a pause button,
wax figured the grown-ups into frozen motions,
open mouthed, wide-eyed, pointing at the sky.
What I know now is that he broke free,
ran to where I squatted in little boy oblivion,
covered me like a carapace as the tree landed
on his back, forced the air out of his lungs,
ground my face in the dirt. Time warped
old memories into the moment. He stood,
breathing hard, steadied himself, like the time
he shrugged the tree off his bruised shoulder,
held me so tight, I didn't want to let him go.

THE CONVERSATION

It's 3 a.m. and we're trapped
in the same nightmare, you perched
on the edge of your bed, pursed lip
breathing, me wondering whether
your heart is racing because of medicine
or if this time you're really dying.

My stomach knots. There are things
I want to tell you, things I hope you know,
things I need you to hear from me,
but now we're sliding on an ice floe,
weighing the risks of another trip
to the ER. Your eyes flare, pupils widen.
You breathe faster, and I know you'd go
if I said the words, but now we're sweating
at a desk on a desert island where we've just signed
our living wills, rolled them into a stoppered bottle
we tossed into the ocean where they've floated
along until this morning, this Saturday
before Father's Day, when I must oxygenate
those thoughts instead of sharing ones
that might bring me peace.

I plunge on. Mom sighs, falls back to her pillow.
Her hand slides across lilacs printed on the bedsheet,
finds yours, squeezes it. Your eyes shine
like they do when grandkids wrap little arms
around you, put their lips to your stone-deaf ears
and whisper everything I want to say.

LUNA: MOON GODDESS

One extra dose of morphine
and the rumor of a moon blends
shadows with truth. A toothless
woman squats in the hall.
Abraham Lincoln's work boots
hang off the bird feeder. A baby
boy rides a little red wagon past
your cedar chest full of medals
and the papers for your GI loan.

I pray for daylight.
You recite the psalms.
The Lord is my Shepherd.
He makes me lie down in green water.
He leads me in the shadow of the valley.
Jesus is coming.

BABY STEPS

Not quite yesterday, not yet tomorrow,
he offered to make coffee.
The percolator burped and gurgled,
quieted the need for conversation
while the kitchen filled with breakfast
smells. I sipped his morning brew
as we stared out the window. The sun
struggled westward toward the mountain.
Coming or going, he asked, then answered
himself. There's no difference in times
like these. He stood, and I shuffled
him back to bed, my hands steady
on his shoulders, learning to walk alone.

DECISION
after Louise Gluck, "The Night Migrations"

This is the moment when
I wish he'd never asked,
the moment when I have
to tell the truth.

It grieves me to think
his glimmer of hope
is an illusion, that he thinks
life might go on.

What will his soul do
when It hears my answer? Stay
a while or punch its ticket,
leave on the next flight.

THE APPOINTMENT

Tap water trickles as you
brace against the sink and dab
a wash cloth at lines and wrinkles
around your eyes.
Your face in the mirror asks
about the time, and when mine
answers, you say something
under your breath as if
being late would mean the end
of the world. I wonder
if being early might postpone it.
My reflection steadies yours
with its hand on your shoulder,
an image of time that has lapsed
too fast, neither of us ready for you to go.

LISTEN TO THE OCEAN

You labor to breathe,
and I ask you to remember
happier times when we sat
by the ocean, mesmerized
by moonlight floating
on the water. It's the highway
to heaven, you used to say.
I watch as peace finds you.
Your respirations slow.
Now and then you pause,
and I count the seconds
until you start again. The tide
is going out. The light
will follow. I will stay
and breathe alone.

DON'T TELL ME WHAT MY DADDY WANTS

Don't sit there
in your starched white coat
with them letters after your name
and squint your big sad eyes.
Don't sing your baby-talk
because you think
it makes me think
you care.

Don't tell me
what "we" need to do,
what he would do for "us,"
what he wants "us" to do for him.
Don't ask me what he'd do
if he only knew
as much as "us,"
as much as you.

Don't wave some
paper at me
where X marks the spot by his printed name
and tell me that's how you know.
Don't say it means
he wouldn't want to eat,
to breathe,
to live this way.

Don't pretend
you understand
two jobs and hungry kids,
rent-to-own furniture,
clothes from Good Will,
one orange for a family of five
at Christmas.

NATURAL DEATH

He looks almost alive, except for the tubes
that sprout from his arms and neck, branch
like vines to form an arbor over his head.
He looks like he's asleep, except for the spout
in his neck that connects to the machine that breathes
for him, which squats next to one that filters poisons
from his blood on Monday, Wednesday and Friday.
He could be dead, but his heart still crawls across
a monitor screen, toward a mirage
that others have imagined for him.
"He's a fighter," one says, as if watching him
circle a squared ring, looking for the chance to land
a crushing body blow, then an uppercut
to death's square jaw. "It's what he'd want,"
says another, shaking his head at the mystery
of anyone who would choose, (if he could),
to stagger from his corner for what is surely
close to the last round, hoping for a win,
even by decision. The walls stand silent
as undertakers. The ventilator sighs.

IT'S NOT THE DYING

It's not the empty, aching, agonal sensation of anguish
from this new part of him that causes pain.

It's not anxiety, apprehension or uncertainty that jerks him up;
pulls him back hard, from the shallow stream of sleep

where he wants to submerge. It's not anger, angst
or apprehension that wakes him, makes him stare

into the darkness, believing that he's dead, wondering
if this is hell. It's not the evasion or erosion of relationships

rendered invalid by this diagnosis. It's not friends who evade
his gaze, avoid his company or appreciate his saying

all is well, thank you, when they know it isn't. It's not regrets
for a wanton, willful, wasted life of good intentions, bad decisions.

It's not the glaring, gaping wound that this decapitation
from his place at the head of his family will create.

It's not the crying they do together when they ponder
the overwhelming, overpowering, inevitability of it.

It's not the dying.

It's the beatific looks of pity as doctors ration five minutes
for a comprehensive review of his complex problems.

It's the double speak of a profession who bemoan a putrid,
paretic, pitiful desire to help, if only they could escape the cold

unfeeling shackles of managed care and restricted formularies.
It's their presumptuous, pious prayers, thanking the God

of the Pharisees that they are not as he is. It's their sanctimonious,
hypocritical insincerity when they ask the God of Mammon

that they be given strength to deal with the contemptible
and minimize their exposure to litigation. It's the faithless,

feral fisted physician who prescribes three days of analgesia,
then makes a return appointment for three months hence.

It's the insouciant, self-satisfied surgeon who counsels
a dying man on the consequences of addiction.

It's the absence of anyone who will believe
that when he says he hurts,

he is truly in pain.

LAST ACT

We both knew it was over.
Pillow fluffed, folded
to fit your aching neck,
the silent smile that followed
my goodbye, routine became
a ceremony of last things.
Shallow breathing measured
your final hour on the stage.

LETTING GO

The house pretends to sleep.
Window shades tremble
against the urge to look.

The porch offers a sad smile.
The doorbell refuses to ring.
Dark soles steal inside.

Black suits wrestle the gurney.
Bedsheets knot, hold ankles.
Door knobs snatch pockets.

English ivy strains to get a grip,
falls limp in mourning.
The limousine tires spin

as it pulls away from the porch.
Dew dampened grass gives
no traction to the truth.

A PROMISE OF REST

Darkness soaks your room.
Silence fills the empty place

in your bed, now twice as big,
half as warm. Your ghost stares

through a winter window
from a black and white photo.

The wind whispers
about another life passing.

You wonder if the sun will rise.
Your heart measures time

in pounding rhythms.
Each beat echoes like a song

sung in an empty church,
a promise, yoked to a memory.

THE LANGUAGE OF GRIEF
after Amy Hempel

Don't leash me with your collars.
Don't stand under your lighter than air phrases
that float in a balloon over your head
then sink under the weight of their own ignorance.

Don't tell me "He's in a better place,"
if you believe that Jesus walked on water,
or "She's not suffering,"
if you're one of the enlightened
who presume that if there is nothing,
it is painless.

Learn from my dog, the one
who perfected the empathic presence
with a wet nose, a wagging tail and silence,
one who is fluent in the language of grief.

RECEIVING FRIENDS

The doctor said you were
an old man's friend,
like you might bring
a covered dish and mingle
in the kitchen with the mourners,
tiptoe in at the wake,
shake hands with the preacher,
sit with the family
and wipe your hollow eyes
with the hem of your cape
when the bugler plays "Taps,"
then go home. Real friends do.
But you still sit in his empty chair
not eating from his plate
that I don't set anymore.
You make me rummage
through his closet, brush
his suits, fold his shirts,
smell the sweat on his hat band,
dust around his briarwood pipes
still waiting on his desk,
dying for a smoke.

BREATHING THE SAME AIR

His hand-carved pipes still lean
in their rack like a row of saxophones
and fill the room with memories
of black vinyl records, Glenn Miller's band
playing "Chattanooga Choo Choo,"
a kitchen match scratched
across the bottom of his shoe
and swirling clouds of tobacco smoke,
a tribute to the charred remains
of the man who still lives in smoke-filled
images of when we breathed the same air.

FAMILY PLOT

A rusted wrought iron fence staggers
around the wrinkled oak
that bows over our family plot,
as if it scattered those graves like seeds,
then expects that drunken cage
to hold them until they are ripe for the harvest.
Its gnarled limbs invite me to sit,
to loosen my tie, empty my pockets
with their gigabytes of memory,
full of names and numbers, places and times,
none important enough to remember.
I sit with those scarred headstones
and listen for the call of songbirds,
a gentle wind on dry branches,
the slap of broad drops on flat leaves,
echoes of mercy, whispers of love.

Thanks

These poems are the precipitate of several sources of inspiration; my dad, who continues to give me life lessons ten years after his death, my team mates in my chapbook poetry writing group whose fingerprints are on many of these poems, our leader, Connie Green, whose gentle coaxing and light touch caused several of these poems to be conceived and finally born, Sue Richardson Orr for hosting us at the Orr Mountain Winery every 3 months for the past several years, my wife Jackie for tolerating my delusions of grandeur, to my daughter Sarah, son Lindsey, daughter-in-law Virginia, grandbabies Audrey Jane and Claire Grace who separately and together make my life worth living.

Ronald H. Lands, MD is a clinical Professor of Medicine at the University of Tennessee, Knoxville where he practices and teaches hematology. He is an MFA alumnus of Queens University of Charlotte, North Carolina. He has work published in anthologies including; *Breathing the Same Air, an Anthology of East Tennessee Writers, Surreal South 2011, an Anthology of Short Fiction, Anthology of Appalachian Writers, Karen Spears Zachiarias, Volume XI, Kakalak 2018*, as well as literary journals including; *New Millennium Writings, Branchwood Journal, Wind, descant, The Distillery, Washington Square, Fourth River, Nassau Review, RiverSedge, the Big Muddy, Floyd County Moonshine, Conte, a Journal of Narrative Writing, Appalachian Heritage, Delta Poetry Review, Intima, a Journal of Narrative Medicine* and others. He has published essays, clinical vignettes and poems from the intersection of writing and medicine in the *Journal of the American Medical Association, Annals of Internal Medicine, Journal of General Internal Medicine, Journal of the American Geriatric Society* and the *Journal of Palliative Medicine*. His work has been nominated for a Pushcart Prize.

www.ingramcontent.com/pod-product-compliance
Lightning Source LLC
LaVergne TN
LVHW041522070426
835507LV00012B/1746